A Practical Guide to Becoming a Nonsmoker

A Practical Guide to Becoming a Nonsmoker

JOSEPH BURKE

iUniverse, Inc.
Bloomington

A Practical Guide to Becoming a Nonsmoker

iUniverse books may be ordered through booksellers or by contacting:

iUniverse
1663 Liberty Drive
Bloomington, IN 47403
www.iuniverse.com
1-800-Authors (1-800-288-4677)

ISBN: 978-1-4620-3031-6 (sc)
ISBN: 978-1-4620-3033-0 (hc)
ISBN: 978-1-4620-3032-3 (ebk)

Printed in the United States of America

iUniverse rev. date: 08/03/2011

CONTENTS

Preface

I am a nonsmoker who, nevertheless, according to Neil Schachter MD in his book *Life and Breath: The Breakthrough Guide to the Latest Strategies for Fighting Asthma and Other Respiratory Problems—At Any Age* (Broadway Books, 2003), still has a twenty-pack-a-year burden on my respiratory system, which is the number of packs per day multiplied by the number of years I smoked. I read Dr. Schachter's book long after quitting my smoking habit, when I was looking for hints to help my wife, who suffers from asthma. In the book, Dr. Schachter outlines some of the assaults and damage caused by smoking, but he also delineates the recovery of organs when smoking has stopped. There is significant recovery, which, of course, is good news.

I started smoking at home about the age of sixteen. Both of my parents had been smokers, although they had given it up at the time. In the late 1950s at the Catholic all-boys high school I attended, one of the privileges that seniors had was the permission to use the smoking lounge during the lunch hour. The lounge was not outfitted with overstuffed chairs, but was rather the top of the concrete stairwell, which had a landing under the roof. On this twenty-five-foot square cement floor, about thirty to fifty students would gather and light up cigarettes. There was no assisted ventilation and it is a wonder that none of us passed out or even that there was enough oxygen concentration to keep the cigarettes burning. We and our smoking habits survived.

Revelation of that "privilege" for seniors seems very strange by today's standards, but that's what it was. I'm sure that privilege was taken away soon after I graduated, but this and others, such as giving away free cigarettes by the tobacco companies to military personnel and to airline customers, show how people were encouraged to continue smoking. Everyone knew that smoking was not good, and we even referred to a cigarette as a "coffin nail." But the push to give up cigarettes was usually a temporary exercise to improve your "wind," which is your endurance during heavy physical activity. Athletes gave up smoking during their seasons and recruits in military service were required to give it up during basic training.

It was in the 1960s that the Surgeon General of the United States declared that smoking was a causative factor in diseases, including cancer. Gradually the push to keep young people from smoking and to get active smokers to quit took hold. This book is a continuation of that push. The hope is that we can turn the tide and help drive a nail into cigarettes' coffin.

I started out writing a "nonsmoking workshop," which I intended to present to smokers who had tried to quit before and then returned to smoking. Perhaps after a few cycles of stopping and starting they might have been discouraged about their ability to break free completely. So I wrote with the idea of encouraging them by carving out a path to follow to become a nonsmoker and including what to do if they started smoking again. The workshop is included in this book. My intention is for you to read through the book and workshop, going back and repeating sections as many times as necessary until you know in your heart that this makes sense and is all you need to give up smoking and substitute a healthier lifestyle of your own choosing. When you decide to give up smoking, you can refer to this book for knowledge and insights that will not only make your task easy and successful but make it a tangible improvement in your life.

Foreword

There is a wealth of information about how to quit smoking. Television, magazines, and the Internet have advertisements and articles about quitting. No doubt everyone is familiar with these, and yet many are still smoking. Perhaps they may not have found a way to convince them that they can successfully quit. Part of the problem can be the sheer amount of material available and the counter-claims for the many products.

The American Cancer Society has a comprehensive, free guide available on the Internet titled "Guide to Quitting Smoking." The information in this file is updated every year. Some interesting points are as follows:

- It is encouraging to learn that in the year 2010 there were more ex-smokers than smokers in the United States (forty-seven million ex-smokers versus forty-six million smokers).
- Typically there is only a 4 to 7 percent chance of being smoke-free after a year for smokers who try to quit by going cold turkey.
- There are many ways to quit smoking. The guide presents both good points and the dangers of several of these methods.
- Using a combination of methods can increase your chances of being successful.

The following list of benefits occur over time after you quit smoking:

a. After twenty minutes your heart rate and blood pressure drop.
b. After twelve hours the carbon monoxide level in your blood drops to normal.
c. After two weeks to three months your circulation improves, and your lung function increases.
d. One year after quitting, the risk of coronary heart disease is half that of a continuing smoker.

e. The risk of stroke can fall to that of a nonsmoker in two to five years.

f. Five years after quitting, the risk of cancer of the mouth, throat, esophagus, and bladder are cut in half. The risk of cervical cancer falls to that of a nonsmoker.

g. Ten years after quitting the risk of dying from lung cancer is about half that of a person who is still smoking.

h. Fifteen years after quitting the risk of coronary heart disease is that of a nonsmoker's.

These statistics are among the good reasons to stop smoking. This book explains many other good reasons.

Introduction

I intend this book to be a practical guide to help smokers get away from their smoking habits. I quit smoking more than thirty years ago, and I have often thought that my experience could help others. I went cold turkey many times before I finally gave up smoking for good. Over the years, by working these thoughts over in my mind, I worked out and refined a method that I call a reasoned approach to quitting smoking. Using a step-by-step procedure, I try to present simple arguments as I understand them in order to get you to accept them and, most importantly, take them to heart. I then offer suggestions that you can take, memorize, and practice until that step is successfully taken. After doing a few steps I hope you will see where this is going and will know that this method can help you achieve the goal of becoming a nonsmoker. I have tried to make this an easy, simple, common-sense approach in contrast to other methods that I feel are unnecessarily prolonged and difficult.

I am not a doctor and my presentations about structures in the human brain and their interactions are meant to be only a common-sense view. While they may not be medically correct, the hope is that the readers will know and feel that the presentation accurately describes what they think is, or, will happen during their attempts to quit smoking. If so, then the suggestions as to how to overcome the problems will make sense and, because they are simple, will be easy to follow.

The neocortex, in the front part of the brain, enables and executes the higher functions: thinking and analysis. One of its main functions is conscious thought. We know that as thoughts are produced they are subjected to analysis and often changed or modified before we accept them. The process can be from fast to slow depending on the complexity of the subject. The limbic system, on the other hand, has evolved to produce fast reactions. The system includes many parts, several of which are located at the top of the brain stem. This has been called the "old brain," as it is the one found in the most primitive animals. One of its functions is to receive inputs from the senses and respond by sending impulses along nerves to muscles. Because our very survival could depend on some of these signals, evolution has designed them to travel very fast. An example is that at the sight of danger, fear will stimulate the limbic system to prepare the body for fight or flight very quickly. Other functions involve learning and memory. Handling these emotional signals are some of the functions of the subconscious mind.

This book is intended to help you no matter how long you have been smoking or how many times you have tried to quit. As you read and understand, you might realize how your habit formed and ensnarled you. If you accept and trust the suggestions, you can counteract the emotional urges to smoke. This will make it much easier to quit and allow you to walk away from your smoking habit.

Quitting the smoking habit is a good end in itself. There is no question about it. However, it can be even more rewarding if you understand the obstacles, make plans to overcome them, and deliberately put these plans into action. You can then see and evaluate their effectiveness and, in the process, gain intimate knowledge of yourself. This is better than just giving up smoking. This is an opportunity to understand and choose to be a person who can evaluate and control their behaviors. When I first started to write the "JSB Nonsmoking Workshop," I wanted to present it as a seminar to a small group of smokers who had previously tried to quit. Quitting can be a "sometime" thing. I have quit successfully several times, and I know that others have done the same. In a small group, I felt that I could make eye contact and tell a more personal story. I wanted to get the audience to buy in to what I was presenting so that, hopefully, I could help them quit smoking. These people identified themselves as smokers, and I was asking them to change their identities even though they knew and trusted who they were. I finally decided that I could ask them to quit, and they could give it a try. Maybe they could even quit for a period of time. They could always go back to smoking if they wanted to do that. That is what I have gone through, and I suspect that is what a lot of folks have gone through. They are the ones who started to smoke from scratch. That is a big jump. After they have given it up for a while that proves they can do it. That makes them the masters. At that point they might think they can just go back and get some relief and a little enjoyment whenever they want, because they can always give it up again. There is a world of temporary smokers out there. This book is a good read for them, as well as for all other smokers and for ex-smokers who might find the reasoned approach here gives them new insights into what they have gone through and achieved.

This book's usefulness might be extended to other users of tobacco products. Chewing tobacco was popular years ago and has made a comeback, particularly with young people. It is another learned habit that, like smoking, with daily repetition through the years can become ingrained. Some of the popularity might be due partly to the many smokers who switched from smoking to chewing. Young men might say they are addicted to chewing and cannot quit. Of course they can quit, but they might be afraid of trying due to fear of failure. You used to see many major league baseball players chewing tobacco on television, but now you see more and more of them chewing gum. That would appear to be a simple, innocuous change. Chewing gum would have few side effects, not counting the good feeling of freshness in your mouth. This book can be a guide for all users of tobacco products, and analogous to the methods presented here, these and other bad habits might yield to a reasoned analysis of how and why they became habits and how to plan to overcome them.

PART ONE:

PRESENTATION

CHAPTER 1

Several Ways to Quit Smoking

A. Cold Turkey

"Cold turkey" is an old phrase. It describes the actions of a person who gives up a habit or addiction all at once, rather than gradually easing the process through gradual reduction or by using replacement medication. Some say the wording was derived from the comparison of the skin of an addict in withdrawal with the appearance of a cold turkey: white with goose bumps (Phrases Dictionary). Cold turkey has also been used as a phrase for food quickly served without much preparation. For someone quitting smoking without preparation another picture may be appropriate. A domestic turkey may be thought of as a bird that is essentially helpless and without direction. The prefix "cold" might imply "out in the cold," which implies without creature comforts. A person attempting to quit by going cold turkey is, in effect, out there wandering around defenseless with the temptations to smoke assailing them. They have only willpower to fight temptations off. Nevertheless, cold turkey is the most common technique, and it is the fastest way to quit smoking.

The ACS "Guide to Quitting Smoking" gives the discouraging statistic that going cold turkey is only successful in 4 to 7 percent of first-time attempts, and, for some it might take eight to ten cycles to be successful. (American Cancer Society 2011). However, I would think that making several attempts would indicate some resolve, and that the percentage of persons successful would increase slightly with additional attempts. In any case, the number of successful persons increases with multiple attempts. I, like millions of others, have given up smoking with multiple cold turkey cycles. And from my personal experience I can say that withdrawal symptoms after four to five cycles are negligible. You can get used to going cold turkey. This could mean that withdrawal symptoms are partially caused by conditioning. After many cycles they really do not bother you.

The conclusion to make is that going cold turkey is not a bad idea, and millions of people can testify to its success. The method costs nothing and does not require you to do or take anything. Starting a cold turkey cycle is the fastest way to quit smoking. Nothing can be faster than being immediately in place as soon as you make up your mind. Perhaps you actually started yesterday (i.e., you may have smoked your last cigarette before you even realized that you were not going to smoke again). I suspect that many times a person might get up in the morning and decide to go cold turkey. Smoking is already past tense for them. Now the only thing required is to get over the withdrawal symptoms and not give in to temptations. It takes a strong will to never give in. And while that might be true, there are a number of aids available to a mind that thinks clearly.

First of all, you got along nicely before you started to smoke. Cigarettes did not bother you then, and, of course, you were not "born to smoke." Your body does not require nicotine to function. This is true regardless of what you think about nicotine addiction. It is proven in every case where someone successfully quits smoking. So in this case, the best thing you can do is to emulate those who have been successful. You could ask people who do not smoke if they have ever been a smoker. Many will tell you that they did smoke. You would probably get a lot of good advice and encouragement from them. But you would instinctively know that it is easy for someone who quit a long time ago to say it was easy to do. They are no longer facing withdrawal symptoms and temptations as you are and will be for some time to come. However you could ask them how long it will be before the headaches, tiredness, and confusion start to go away. It may well be shorter than you think.

It is actually not true, but you probably think that only a cigarette will take these symptoms away. Part of the reason is that during withdrawal, you get tired and it is difficult to get your mind cleared up. When you feel this way, it is a good time to take a nap, if you can. Your body is telling you what it needs. Taking a nap would be the best medicine for you. When you are tired, the mind does not work efficiently. Inputs start to pile up faster than the mind can decide what to do with them. Then, like a computer bogging down, the overload puts a huge drag on how your mind handles things. If this goes on, you get more tired, and your mental acuity goes way down. This happens to everyone at the end of the day. The solution is to get some sleep. During sleep the input is closed off while the mind sorts out all the things that have been piling up. You wake up refreshed, with things in good order, ready to start a new day or the rest of your day, able to receive and process new input.

However, when you are trying to give up a strong habit, the subconscious mind feeds up requests to the conscious mind to engage the habitual routine. The conscious mind can reject the idea, but it cannot get away from the subconscious mind. The request is soon sent up again. This banter keeps up, continually interrupting the conscious mind, which has to decide what to do with the request. What happens is that the conscious mind realizes that these requests are coming frequently. This causes the conscious mind to begin to wonder whether to grant the request. It begins to take longer and require more thought to reject the request from the subconscious mind. The conscious mind starts to get behind in handling inputs and decisions from other sources. Inputs start building up and you get tired and confused. Finally, you give in and start to agree that you "need" a cigarette. This may not be medically correct, but it is a reasonable way to imagine what is happening to you.

There is a silver lining in this bag of difficulties, and it is getting closer. Your worst day of withdrawal will probably be the first day. After you have spent a day rejecting the emotional signals that cause you to think you want a cigarette, you may be starting to get better at rejecting these signals. The silver lining is that you can start to teach your subconscious mind that you do not like these suggestions. You can tell your habit that you do not want to be bothered anymore. You can also start to change the urge to something that you would like to do or to think about. You can begin to take control! This can definitely start to feel good. In addition the withdrawal symptoms will be decreasing rather quickly over time. The first day of withdrawal symptoms is the greatest outside shock to your system. The day before, you might have smoked twenty cigarettes or more. This day you will smoke none. You would expect that to be a shock to your system, and it is. The next day, however, will be the same as the last one. You will not smoke a single cigarette, and that routine is the same as the day before. Furthermore, the amount of nicotine in your body is decreasing every day. In three to four days the nicotine should be completely washed out of your system, and you will most likely feel better as you breathe only clean air and the poisons are being washed out through the kidneys. You will find that the only problems are the temptations that come up as a result of habit from your subconscious mind and, of course, suggestions and invitations from your smoking friends. You need to tell them that you are trying to get over your smoking habit, and ask them for their help and encouragement. How to handle temptations from your subconscious mind is one of the main topics in the JSB Nonsmoking Workshop in Part II of this book.

B. Hypnosis

The easiest way to quit smoking is through hypnosis. It is easy because it takes a minimum of willpower, and the withdrawal symptoms are very mild or nonexistent. Hypnosis is an old art that has been portrayed in carnivals and shows as an esoteric ability to take over a person's mind and control that person. That, of course, is a false understanding. Hypnosis is an art that takes advantage of the way our brains have developed and the way they work. Different parts of the brain do different functions. The conscious mind performs the cognitive functions. It is the thinking, analytical part of the brain. The subconscious mind is where routine functions are handled. For example, the subconscious mind controls the muscles that modulate the flow of air in our windpipes and makes speech possible. This and other subconscious programs are called up and run by emotional signals coming through the limbic system. When we want to do something, the subconscious mind starts and runs the parade of programs to accomplish the task. Sometimes we need to respond very quickly (e.g., when we need to duck to avoid being hit by a flying object). For this reason, signals coming through the limbic system travel very fast. Hypnosis is a developed art that recognizes the separation of functions. You might think of it like a computer virus. If you can plant a program in the subconscious mind, you can call it up later on. The hypnotist offers suggestions for you to store in your subconscious mind. You are in charge of your own mind. The hypnotist can only offer suggestions. The key is for the hypnotist to get your approval to store the suggestions. The approval must come through the conscious mind, which handles the thinking and deciding functions. If the conscious mind can be sufficiently relaxed, the suggestions can get through and be stored in the subconscious mind.

A simple description is that while awake the conscious mind is busy receiving input from the five senses, sorting out which input signals to think about and their order of importance. These are the discerning, analytical functions of the brain. The subconscious mind is the activity part of the brain. Thus the brain has separate sections for thinking and for doing. A lot of the doing part is called into action by emotions. If you want to stand up, the subconscious brain calls up the program for the bodily movements to perform that task. Once the program is stored, it only requires a minimum of thinking to perform that task. This allows the conscious mind to keep working independently. You can stand up and at the same time continue with your conversation. The separation of different parts of the brain for different functions is very efficient. However, it requires amazing coordination to carry out these tasks simultaneously. One help is the storage of routine programs in the subconscious mind. In a newborn baby we see those programs being developed and stored. The baby first learns to move and control his arms and legs. Then he moves his body, crawls, and pulls himself up to a standing position. There he works on developing the coordination of the muscles to keep himself balanced. Finally, he learns to walk. All the while he is storing these routines in the subconscious mind to be used when he gets the urge to move or walk.

The beginning smoker does the same thing, learning the physical, mental, and psychological ways to find relaxation and pleasure in smoking. These routines, stored in the subconscious mind, are called up by the emotion seeking pleasure or relaxation and perceived as the thought, *I want to smoke*. This is the emotional basis of your smoking habit.

In a former time it was said that the hypnotist would put the subject "to sleep." The true description is that the person's conscious mind is relaxed by monotonous repetition to the point where, like a sleepy sentry, he lets suggestions into the subconscious mind that he would ordinarily hold up or question. The hypnotized person is highly susceptible to suggestions. The conscious mind under hypnosis does not interfere, criticize, analyze, or scrutinize the suggestions as it would when fully awake. In this state the hypnotist can make suggestions to the subconscious mind to change or suppress the habit of smoking. However, the person under hypnosis has not given up, put to sleep, or compromised his or her conscience, free will, or moral direction. They can accept, reject, or modify any suggestion that goes against what they really want to do. Sometimes the hypnotherapist will plant the seed of an idea and in later sessions will be able to convince the person to accept the suggestions.

A typical suggestion that the hypnotist may offer is "when you wake up you will no longer want to smoke." Notice the simplicity and directness of the suggestion. The person is told that he can just directly become a nonsmoker. The suggestion is that almost miraculously he can leap over all the willpower battles and the withdrawal symptoms and simply find himself in the land of the nonsmoker. Can this giant step actually be taken? The answer is "yes" only if the person accepts the suggestion and is willing to allow the suggestion to spring up emotionally in response to any temptation to smoke. Under hypnosis the person can accept the suggestion and easily take that giant leap. We can see why it may take several sessions, and that there will be differences in the effectiveness of hypnosis depending on the receptivity of the person. But we can also see that hypnosis goes directly to the solution of the problem. It is the easiest way to change or modify a behavior or habit.

If you look up information about hypnosis, you will find that every hypnotic trance is self-induced and controlled. Furthermore, hypnosis does not put you into a weird trance. It is, in fact, the kind of state we get into when we watch a good movie or are absorbed in any comforting activity that lets our conscious mind relax and our subconscious mind play out familiar routines, openly accepting suggestions. We spend a good deal of relaxing time in these states that are similar to hypnotic trances.

Training in self hypnosis is the subject of many self-help books and tapes to overcome bad habits, increase self-confidence, lose weight, or develop good habits. The procedures tell you to sit in a comfortable chair in a warm, quiet room where you will be safe, alone, and uninterrupted, a place where you can relax and go to sleep without fear or concern. There are a series of relaxation procedures that relax both the muscles and the attention of the conscious mind. If planned out and done right, you will have set up your subconscious mind to accept suggestions that are not against your conscience or core beliefs. Talking intimately then to your subconscious mind, you can lay out the most gentle and previously thought-out behavioral modifications. Self-hypnosis books contain guidelines about what to say. At the end of the session you bring the conscious mind back to attention and relax and absorb the full feelings of warmth, safety, truth, and acceptance. Repeat often until the subconscious mind fully accepts and reprograms itself to the best possible behaviors. This is as gentle, intimate, desirable, and rewarding as it gets and, as a bonus, it can be a lot of fun.

In a one-sentence statement the ACS guide states that studies have not supported hypnosis as a method that works (American Cancer Society 2011). One possibility is that those who quit with the help of hypnosis might have a high rate of relapse. For some, hypnosis may be so easy that they fail to put any personal effort into quitting and staying smoke free. This book will stress that you can not be successful if you do not want to quit and are not willing to put some determination into the effort. Obviously, more studies need to be done. I personally know people who tried to quit cold turkey several times and were finally able to quit with the help of hypnosis. The key is that it is a painless, easy way and, although it may take more than one session, it can be successful. Whatever method you choose, it is a certainty that if you want to and do not give up, you will succeed. Smoking and its grip on you is not mysterious or bigger than life, and it is certainly not bigger than your own free will. What you want to do in this regard, you can do. However, quitting smoking is only half of the project; the other half is staying smoke free for the long haul.

In the Workshop, I outline a path to become a nonsmoker, one who is not tempted to smoke. I think this is best accomplished by quitting on your own without relying on external aids, because the temptation to relapse might be there when the aids are discontinued. In contrast, if you quit on your own, you will probably be stronger with more resolve rather than be vulnerable to continuing temptations.

C. Medicinal Aids
a. Nicotine Replacement Therapy (NRT)

Medicinal nicotine is available in many forms to replace the nicotine that you take in from smoking. The object of NRT is to avoid or lessen the withdrawal symptoms when you begin to quit. This makes quitting easier and encourages many more smokers to take the plunge. The results of many studies indicate that all forms of NRT are effective, and that 25 to 33 percent of participants are successful in being smoke free after six months (American Cancer Society 2011). These results, like the 4 to 7 percent success by cold turkey attempts, show that it takes some determination and possibly several attempts to actually conquer the habit for good. The lesson here is to not get discouraged if an attempt does not succeed. The many studies of NRT have shown that nicotine replacement is one and a half to two times more effective than a placebo. Using the midranges of these studies, it appears that cold turkey is about 5 percent successful, placebo therapy is about 17 percent successful, and NRT is about 29 percent successful. These numbers are probably pretty good as they are the averages of many studies. Nicotine replacement is the most successful. However, even the regimen of taking a placebo triples your chances of success over just going cold turkey. We can get a lot of insight from these numbers. Many millions of people have quit smoking by going cold turkey, and yet this is the least effective way. The regimen of taking a placebo surprisingly triples your chances. This shows that there is definitely both a nicotine addiction and a mental component to your habit.

There are many NRT products, including patches, gums, nasal sprays, inhalers, and lozenges. It is your own choice which one you select, however you should discuss this with your doctor. You need a prescription for nasal sprays and inhalers. But for every method there are possible side effects, and it is advisable to see a doctor before and during the therapy. The doctor will be able to advise you on the effectiveness of your treatment and how to cope with side effects if they occur. There is also a danger of overuse (using much more than the prescribed amount). NRT is a temporary treatment designed to get you over the unpleasant part of quitting. Using too much is a danger particularly with the as-needed types of delivery such as gums, sprays, and inhalers. The FDA has approved each method for a certain limited time. There is a real danger of getting addicted to any of these methods. Your doctor can determine if you are susceptible to this danger and help you avoid it. One statistic shows that 15 to 20 percent of those who quit with the help of nicotine gum are still using the gum a year later (American Cancer Society 2011). There is also the possibility of a relapse when the nicotine therapy is stopped.

I personally do not recommend NRT because of possible side effects and possibility of addiction. In addition, I think they take the emphasis off of a most important part of your addiction, which is the emotional source of the urge to smoke. The literature mentions that there is a mental component to your smoking habit and that you should deal with it. However, the assumption for using NRT is that the big and lasting component is the nicotine addiction.

Smokers develop a physical dependence on continuing the smoking habit. The mechanism for this has been studied. Nicotine receptors have been identified in the brain. When stimulated these sites release chemicals that produce pleasure and/or a feeling of well-being. These sites are not exclusively for nicotine. There are many chemicals carried in the blood that flows through the brain. To have any effect or communication with the brain certain chemicals, neurotransmitters, must be able to cross the blood-brain barrier. The barrier is a selective filter. The nicotine molecule is of the size and shape that it can cross the barrier and stimulate a pleasure site in the brain. The first puff of smoke produces some pleasure and is quite satisfying. Apparently the body and brain get used to this amount of nicotine for the next spike of pleasure does not come until you increase the concentration of nicotine with the next puff of smoke. The pleasure realized is decidedly less with each succeeding puff. The interested reader can find much more on this subject. However, I know that many ex-smokers did not have much, if any, trouble that they associated with nicotine receptors prolonging their addiction. Withdrawal symptoms were real and, as I have mentioned several times, they make you feel uncomfortable. However, they go away in a few days and never return. Nicotine replacement can be counterproductive if it prolongs your dependence on nicotine. You can view it as similar to a cat playing with a victim rather than killing it quickly. The real trouble as I see it is that concentrating on nicotine changes the emphasis from where it should be which is on the emotional addiction. The literature mentions mental addiction and then tells you that nicotine withdrawal is a problem but that it is usually short-lived. So why is it necessary to treat it for a long time? I think the best way is to get over it quickly and be done with it.

Nicotine addiction is both a physical and a mental addiction. The mental addiction comes from the association of pleasure derived from smoking with tobacco. That is just a misplaced association. This will be covered in detail in the workshop in Part Two of this book.

b. Prescription Drugs

There are non-nicotine drugs that are available for smoking cessation. This section lists and describes them.

i) Bupropion (Zyban® or Wellbutrin®) are antidepressants in extended-release form. They act on chemicals in the brain that are related to cravings for nicotine. You start taking them one to two weeks before starting to quit smoking. You can use them in conjunction with NRT. Discuss this with the doctor writing the prescription.

ii) Varenicline (Chantix) works by interfering with nicotine receptors in the brain to lessen the pleasures of smoking and to reduce nicotine withdrawal symptoms. You start taking one pill per day one week before quitting smoking. The treatment lasts for twelve weeks, and the prescribing doctor can extend that time. The prescribed regimen for using these drugs is to be followed. There are possible serious side effects if not used as prescribed. It is necessary to taper down before stopping these drugs. Consult your doctor for specific details (American Cancer Society 2011).

I recently saw an addiction expert on TV telling an interviewer that cocaine is not addictive, because most users do not become addicted. That is obviously true of alcohol as well. If these powerful agents are not addictive, how much power can nicotine have over you? It is you who started this by letting yourself think that smoking is a "pleasure." But where exactly does that pleasure come from? The first puff of smoke that you inhale is the best. After that, with each puff the pleasure decreases and by the end of the cigarette the distaste for smoke is on the increase. I suggest that the pleasure is not from the smoke or the nicotine but from the relief of getting the signals from your subconscious mind to quit hounding you. The most important thing to realize is that you do not have to give up any pleasure when you quit smoking. You can still get the pleasure and relaxation associated with it by substituting healthy and uplifting techniques in place of the urge to smoke. Realizing what is really bothering you can make it much easier to get over the smoking addiction. I will cover this in the workshop.

D. Motivational Resources

There are many sources for help and motivation, including classes and seminars for quitting smoking. Nicotine Anonymous is a twelve-step program similar to the one for alcoholics. The American Lung Association offers adult and teen programs for quitting smoking. Family, friends, co-workers and ex-smokers are good sources for advice and encouragement. Seek out all the help you can get. Every idea can help you build a defense against the mental slavery of addiction. Most will tell you that the pleasure of smoking is a misnomer. Any pleasure experienced was not due to nicotine or to the cigarette, but was entirely the pleasure that you produced yourself. As an illustration, consider the pleasure that a clown gets from entertaining an audience. First the clown makes up a routine and practices every step. Before going on-stage, he puts on a costume and applies an overabundance of makeup. In the performance, he measures out the sequences, timing, and feedback for maximum audience participation. The laughter and amusement is the result of the clown's performance; the costume has nothing to do with it. Oh, you may disagree, but look a little closer. The costume is for the audience's perception. It helps them perceive and understand the humor of the clown's actions. They laugh and applaud, which in turn produces the clown's pleasure. The clown was funny or not and that was independent of the costume. The cigarette may be your costume, but your pleasure is quite independent of it.

E.   Counseling

There are professional counselors who specialize in helping people get over their smoking habits. You can find them through the health departments where you work or attend school, or in the city where you live. There is free telephone-based counseling service available in all fifty states and in the District of Columbia. Operators can put you in touch with trained counselors. And, of course, there are counselors you can talk to for a fee. The help they provide probably varies greatly from place to place and from patient to patient.

CHAPTER 2

Why You Smoke

You are a smoker now. You are about to make a decision as to whether you will be a smoker forever—or will you, as many others before you have done, decide to walk away from your smoking habit? Before you make that decision it might be a good idea to sit down and think about what makes you smoke. You are addicted to a habit. You cannot make it through the day without a cigarette. You probably cannot last more than an hour without one. You identify yourself as a smoker; others do too. What is it that has you so tightly in its grip that you cannot break free? You will find that it is absolutely nothing that you did not put there.

Let's look at some of the common triggers that make people automatically reach for a cigarette. Perhaps you find that when you are stressed you think a cigarette would help you get your bearings. But let's be a little more analytical. Recall how this happens. When you are stressed and you start to get tired, you look for a place to sit down. You go into a mechanical mode. You reach inside your pocket or purse and get out a pack of cigarettes. You take one out, tamp it down, and put it to your lips. You get out a match or lighter, strike it, put the flame to the tip of the cigarette, inhale to draw the fire into the cigarette, and then take the smoke into your mouth and lungs. As you exhale, you feel the little impact in your chest and the spike in blood pressure. It feels so comforting, so familiar. You feel the stress melting away. But how does this work?

Think about what drives you to become ensnared in this habit. You say, "Nicotine, I am addicted to nicotine." That is what you might have been told, and what many before you have also been told. However, I personally think nicotine is a minor part of your addiction. Addiction is what you have let it become. Let's look back analytically over the scenario. You've read about hypnosis. You know that the conscious mind can wear itself down making decisions when overloaded. It might have been one of those days when things were happening just too fast. You became a little tired and weary. Your subconscious mind had been trained to suggest that you might feel better if you smoke a cigarette. You accepted the suggestion and found in the little familiar routine of getting and smoking a cigarette that the conscious mind was given a rest as you deliberately did not receive inputs requiring a lot of thought. But let's be honest. You almost deliberately set this scenario up as you started to get tired by constantly saying to yourself, "I need a cigarette." To get into a hypnotic trance you are made to relax and the conscious mind is presented with a monotonous repetition of very simple inputs. There are no spikes in the incoming information. You feel comfortable knowing there will be no inputs that require immediate attention. Your mind can fixate on harmless repetition. The conscious mind relaxes and the subconscious mind is brought into play. With your little habitual routine, like the one described above, you have started a kind of hypnotic trance. It's a little routine that you've repeated over and over through the days and the years. The conscious mind can start to relax and the subconscious mind can be opened up to suggestions. Now you see that you have stacked the deck. You have been saying for a long time, "If only I had a cigarette." At least half of the problem and the solution was your own deliberate doing. You made this thing work. Nicotine produced a little spike in blood pressure, and the taste and the feeling of a slight impact in your chest were familiar. However, it was the resting of the conscious mind and the familiarity of the routine that allowed you to relax and relieve the stress.

There is another factor that you falsely think is working for you. You think the banter between your subconscious mind and your conscious mind has been cleared up. I will go over this in detail in the workshop. But for now, you realize that the pressure from your habit is not resolved. It will come again to get you to take time out for a cigarette. You gave in this one time, but that is definitely not the end of it. You will be tempted again. Perhaps you think the spike that nicotine produced helped you in this situation. However, as an exercise, let your mind go over some other inputs that would produce a little spike. If there was a sudden loud noise that might cause a little spike in blood pressure, but would it do anything to relieve stress? Think of something else that might have a little impact in your chest and make your blood pressure spike. Consider if that would help. Work this out for yourself. It's good to figure out for yourself exactly what that cigarette did to make you feel better.

You are paying for it. What did it actually do for you? My guess is that the relaxation and familiarity of your little routine are responsible for the stress relief. Note well that you do not have to smoke to enjoy them.

There are other common triggers that people actually look for to remind them that it would be a good time to smoke. Perhaps you use a cigarette to gather your thoughts. Or maybe you just like to relax with your cigarette. You might think that the cigarette is your friend because it increases your self confidence. Perhaps it gives you an added boost when you need one. Or finally you might use your habit to be part of the gang, meet new people, break the ice, or spend time with friends or co-workers. In any or all of these cases it would be helpful to examine them to see what you do and what your habit does. Look at your cigarette or habit as a separate person. Come out of your body and look down on the two of you, you and your cigarette. Go through a typical scenario. If the cigarette made you feel more comfortable, think of how much freer and more comfortable you would feel if you did not need that cigarette. You know that the cigarette is an extraneous need and distraction. And the cigarette did not do any of the talking or thinking or reacting. It did not remember anything for you. You took all the risks and you deserve all the credit. Do not think that your little friend burning up in your fingers deserves any credit at all. You deserve the credit because you have worked out a routine to settle down an overactive conscious mind by calling up these simple steps that are in your subconscious mind. Your habit gives structure and pattern to an overloaded mind. It brings familiarity to a situation that you might be trying to figure out. The stress goes away as you realize that you can calm down and figure these things out.

You can get a lot of help for yourself if you do not give up on this process. It can be helpful and really a lot of fun. You can apply the suggestions just outlined to other little routines or habits. You might think about how you meet friends or strangers. Are you generally upbeat and happy to meet them, or do you try to avoid seeing them? What do you do when someone monopolizes the conversation? How do you face work or study obligations? Think about some of your habitual routines, the way you approach them, and the actions you typically perform. Then begin to look at them objectively. Some of them you will like and feel good about. Others you might decide you want to revise or change. You are your own coach here. Step out of yourself and watch how you do things. See what makes you feel good, and then see how you can make some adjustments. As you do this time and again you might find better ways to handle situations. As you make little changes that make you feel better, you will become more self confident. First of all, you realize that the cigarette or any other crutch does not add anything to the way a situation turns out.

There is a mathematical technique called *iteration* that computer programs use in calculations. A guess or approximation is made and the calculation is performed. The answer is compared to a standard or known answer. Using the difference a better guess is made and fed into the calculation, which is run again. A simple example is how the square root of a number can be obtained by making an estimate. To find the square root of a number, N, make an estimate, "a", that is fairly close. If "a" is not the exact answer, calculate a new estimate as $á = ½ (a + N/a)$. This new estimate will be much closer if not exactly right. Continue making new estimates until the correct answer is achieved. The series converges on the right answer very quickly.

The point to be made is that there is continuous improvement that leads to the right answer. You can use the same technique to help unravel your smoking habit. Take a small step and see if there is improvement. For example, you have probably been accepting almost any invitation or temptation to smoke. Now you might decide to pass up one of these invitations. When you do, remind yourself that this is how you gain control. Reject the idea that you are passing up some pleasure. You are not missing any; you are transferring that pleasure to the realization that you are taking control. When you see that there was improvement, and you were pleased with the result, plan and take another small step. Let the results embolden you to keep going. Each cycle that gets you closer to where you want to be convinces you that you are on the right path. Do not get tired or impatient; just be happy to be making progress. And when I say be happy, I intend to imply that you can actually have fun planning and executing these steps and measuring how much progress you have made. Your habit is there. It is a real thing that you are trying to conquer. You are the warrior going after it. Plan your conquests and feel the satisfaction of getting the upper hand. You will definitely feel better about it, and I would say you can have fun doing it. When a temptation comes do not just say "no" and then feel you missed some pleasure, instead you can choose to say, "I am not doing that anymore." Feel good that you have asserted yourself. Take a deep breath and don't forget to smile. It will be good for you.

CHAPTER 3

A New Way to Quit: The Reasoned Approach

Hypnosis is the easiest way to give up smoking, but it may take several sessions during which the subject will probably continue to smoke, maybe a little less, but still continue as a smoker. Going cold turkey is the fastest way to quit smoking but it can be difficult, and it could well take several attempts to finally be able to quit for good. The trouble here is that there may be long lapses in between the cold turkey cycles. Is there an easier, quicker way to quit smoking? This book addresses that problem by pointing out a good opportunity to reprogram the subconscious mind by a reasoned approach. In hypnosis the conscious mind is relaxed so that the subconscious mind is easily addressed and suggestions for improved behavior can be easily fed in. It is much harder and less efficient, they say, to offer suggestions to the conscious mind, which is busy receiving input, analyzing that information, and deciding what to do with it. In this state, the conscious mind does not need superfluous suggestions meant for the subconscious mind.   With the conscious mind being worked that much harder, the person can get both tired and upset. His or her mind will get tired because with these interruptions, it will have to work harder than normal, and the person will get upset because things are not going as smoothly and easily as they normally would. This leads to inefficiency, as the suggestions meant for reprogramming the subconscious mind might not be stored in the most effective place. In the worst-case scenario the information may just be lost. However, there is an opportunity here for a method that is as easy as hypnosis, and with the immediacy of going cold turkey. This is what I call the "reasoned approach." We have all heard a good lecture during which our conscious minds were very much alert, and we could easily grasp and store the information. Using our analytical thought process, we can recall and use that information even years later. This is with analytical thought. It is also possible to present reasoned arguments to the conscious mind that can be efficiently passed on to the subconscious mind in the form of suggestions for behavioral modifications. Let us suppose you often jaywalk at a particular point on a street. One day a policeman standing nearby tells you that if you do it again he will most definitely give you a ticket. For the next two or three days you glance down the street and see him standing there looking at you. It is a good bet that you will voluntarily change your behavior. This is a case where the change was pushed, but you can probably come up with examples that convince you that behavioral change can as easily be pulled into your patterns. What if you saw a person you knew buying a lottery ticket at a certain location and then later finding out that they had purchased a winning ticket? We clearly do act on suggestions that come through our conscious mind. The danger that they may be forgotten, rejected or changed does exist, but the way to minimize that is to get the subject, while alert and conscious, to "buy in" to the suggestions. Then the conscious mind recognizes these as good ideas and readily feeds them to the subconscious mind where they can be absorbed and effect changes in behavioral habits. This is the reasoned approach.

The key is to present information that people can receive with their hearts. Their emotions will tell them this is simple, true, and applicable to their needs. This is the approach I use in the JSB Nonsmoking Workshop. The seven steps of the workshop outline a path to quitting your smoking habit. Each step is written as an appeal to think out what would be involved in your particular case and plan to make this a step toward freedom. This is really a form of self-hypnosis with the suggestions for behavioral modification already written for you. You have to read the suggestions and understand that they make sense and be able to apply them to your situation. Then you can take them to heart and with a feeling think, *This is what I want to do, and I really can do it.* Then you can act on the suggestions, and as you practice, improve on them with your own ideas. You will be able to enjoy the progress you are making, and you will find that giving up smoking can really be fun.

After you read all of the steps, you can work on internalizing the process. To accomplish this, you can go over each step, working on what it means and what changes it can bring into your life. The thing I want to accomplish is to get your "buy in" into the process. I want you to think and reflect on your life, your hopes, and what you want to do and become. Each little step is something you can do. When you add up the little steps, you will see that you have accomplished a great deal. You will have built a new you.

This is not a little thing. The workshop breaks down the task of becoming a nonsmoker into doable little steps. In our lives things can get complicated. Smoking has probably gotten complicated in your own life. You have probably internalized the "pleasures" of smoking that the media advertises. You might look forward to taking a break from work or studies to meet with friends for conversation and relaxation. Oops! I left out smoking! Of course, when you think about it, smoking is just an excuse to get together. The real pleasure is being with friends, laughing, and relaxing. Smoking really has nothing to do with it. My father told me a story that illustrates this diversionary technique in selling. A traveling salesman was selling vacuum cleaners. He called at a house and was let in to demonstrate the vacuum cleaner. He turned the machine on and started to vacuum the rug. The woman who lived there had to scream at him to be heard. He turned the cleaner off, and she said, "My God, that makes a terrible racket!" He said, "Yes m'am, it's very powerful." We have put up with the terrible "racket" of smoking because we think it is a powerful relaxant for us, but it is nothing of the sort. The pleasure and good times are from being with our friends and the good cheer we share. These powerful relaxants do not depend on smoke and will certainly be there whether we smoke or not.

In our social lives we weave these things together and the results can "complicate" things. By using a process of analyzing each little step and then seeing how things fit together, we can see how to control some of these "complicated" things. Psychologists and advisors make a good living by helping people unravel the complications in their lives. Hopefully, this process can help you unravel the challenge of how to quit smoking. Becoming a nonsmoker is the answer. It is as simple as that. You have to decide that you want to quit, and then look for ways to accomplish each little step. It can be an eye-opener, and it can be fun and exciting. You can get to work on it now.

CHAPTER 4

You Are Who You Think You Are

The statement "you are who you say you are" is true only on a limited basis. It is not true if you say that you are a high-school teacher but have no qualifications and have never been employed as one. However, it can potentially be true if you are talking about your personality, behavioral habits, or goals. You can use it as an expression of determination. In particular, you can say that you are an ex-smoker if you are determined to be one. In contrast, it does not convey the correct meaning to say that you are a smoker if you firmly intend not to smoke anymore. The value here for the person trying to give up smoking is that they can start to behave like an ex-smoker and begin to get friends used to the fact. If people do not think you are a smoker, they will not invite you out to the alley to have a smoke. They will not offer you a cigarette. Even before you give up smoking, you can start to become an ex-smoker. This will help your friends get used to it, and it will give you the opportunity to find out some of the good things about not smoking.

There are positive things you can start to do along these lines. Let's face it, smoking is obnoxious even if you say you like it and feel addicted to it. The by-products are fire, smoke, and ashes, none of which are appealing. You most probably do not like secondhand smoke, even your own. You know it can be harmful to those around you. The sight and smell of tar and residue from tobacco smoke is disgusting. You can begin to clean up by emptying and washing ashtrays. It's a little chore and they will get filled up again, but give yourself a moment to look and realize that you somehow feel better when the tray is clean. Straighten out the pack of cigarettes and place it in a spot rather than just throwing it on the table. You can even put the cigarettes out of sight just to see how it will look when you never have a need for them again. Smoke does permeate clothing and fabrics. Get some of them dry cleaned and see if this makes you feel good. The pack, matches, and other smoking implements are really extra things that you lug around. Deliberately leave them home when you go to the store or for a short trip. Think about how it would make you feel better or at least relieved if you didn't have to worry about these things. If you use air fresheners to cover up the smoke, think of the freedom you could have if there was no smoke. You could choose a milder, more delicate scent and enjoy it more. When the people in the office go out for a smoke, pass it up once and do something else that you enjoy. It could be some relaxing technique, a prayer, a meditation, or making a personal call—any thing that appeals to you. Look around for people you would like to associate with who do not smoke. This is definitely not to get away from your smoking friends. Just the opposite, you are just starting something that one day you can encourage them to follow. It is a positive step for you and, if they follow your example, it will be better for them, as well.

CHAPTER 5

How Emotional Intelligence Can Help You Curb
a Harmful Habit

Emotional intelligence is equally as important as IQ intelligence as tested by reasoning, mathematic, reading, language, and memory skills. The former are recognized and form the basis of children's education, while emotional intelligence skills are largely ignored (Goleman 1997). Yet, how well we perform in daily life is largely dependent on the way we recognize and handle what our emotions are telling us. We intuitively understand this at least in the extreme. For example, we know that rage or anger can take over and put a person out of control. Goleman mentions data that show by imaging techniques that in extremely emotional situations the limbic system, which handles emotional signals can hijack the brain not allowing the reasoning processes to get started or to come into play. The emotional system, by design, is powerful enough to completely take over the brain. However, we do have control if we teach ourselves to control it. The urge to smoke is an emotional signal. It comes in the form of the suggestion, "I want to smoke." Just realizing these connections gives us power to learn how to control these suggestions. Emotional intelligence provides a powerful tool for living a happy and productive life and, in this particular instance; it can help us change the desire to smoke into a determination to develop better behaviors for a significant improvement in our lives.

Researchers have defined emotional intelligence as "the ability to perceive emotion, integrate emotion to facilitate thought, understand emotions, and to regulate emotions to promote personal growth" (Mayer et al. 2001. 232–242). An ability-based model views emotions as useful sources of information that help us to make sense of and navigate the social environment. This ability manifests itself in certain adaptive behaviors. This model claims that emotional intelligence includes the following four types of abilities (Salovey 1997):

1. Perceiving emotions—the ability to detect and decipher emotions in faces, pictures, voices, and cultural artifacts, including the ability to identify one's own emotions. Perceiving emotions represents a basic aspect of emotional intelligence, as it makes all other processing of emotional information possible.
2. Using emotions—the ability to harness emotions to facilitate various cognitive activities, such as thinking and problem solving. The emotionally intelligent person can capitalize fully upon his or her changing moods in order to best fit the task at hand.
3. Understanding emotions—the ability to comprehend emotion language and to appreciate complicated relationships among emotions. For example, understanding emotions encompasses the ability to be sensitive to slight variations between emotions, and the ability to recognize and describe how emotions evolve over time.
4. Managing emotions—the ability to regulate emotions in both ourselves and in others. Therefore, the emotionally intelligent person can harness emotions, even negative ones, and manage them to achieve intended goals.

I included the information above just to introduce the concept and definition of emotional intelligence. For smoking cessation the ideas behind two of these abilities can be most helpful. The recognition of the ability to use emotions in the best way for the task at hand is one more source of power. The ability of the emotionally intelligent person to regulate and manage their own emotions to achieve intended goals is a very useful, powerful, and desirable trait. *You can harness the power of the emotion that calls you to smoke and direct it to a more productive goal.* Do not reject this idea or say that it is hard or impossible. Reread the sentence and let the idea begin to sink in. Nurture it, and it will make your task a happy and much easier one. This is one of the main ideas that I develop in the workshop. What you need to understand now is the emotional nature of the urge to smoke and that you can learn to manage this urge and make it work for you. When the urge comes to you, do you feel in control of it? Probably yes, at least for a little while. However, the urge does not completely go away. You might suppress it, but it remains unresolved in your subconscious mind. The urge will come back on schedule and remind you that it has been even longer since you have had a cigarette. This cycle will be repeated until you finally give in. Obviously, you will be in this fight with yourself unless you break the cycle.

Understand the emotional nature of the suggestions. Nicotine has very little or nothing at all to do with it. Perhaps you have given up smoking before and after a period of time you came back to your habit. Nicotine washes out of the system in a few days. That stuff was long gone and still you came back to smoking again. Was it nicotine receptors in the brain that continued to request some sustenance? As an excuse, we look too hard for a physical reason for our addiction. That, I think, is because we feel that a physical reason is stronger and more persistent than an emotional one, and we feel that a physical source can be medically treated so that we do not have to tax our willpower. We lose a great opportunity with this kind of thinking. First of all, an emotional urge can be much more persistent. Have you ever heard of anyone saying the words, "I will love you forever"? Obviously you can readily think of many emotions that can be very persistent and they can be very strong as well. So that part of the argument does not hold. What about the physical source being more amenable to treatment? That is entirely up to you. I'll try my persuasion by the fact that with any medicinal treatment there are side effects that can be dangerous. You can get much faster and more direct relief by recognizing and treating the emotional source. In addition, you can pretty much select the side effects you want and, in particular, you can select ones that will lead to good, positive, and happy results in your life. When you stand there and look either backward or forward you can realize that, lo and behold, this is a great opportunity.

So how do you go about recognizing and using these abilities? I don't know as I am not a trained expert, but I can offer some common sense approaches. Some of the emotions we feel include fear, anger, happiness, joy, sadness, longing, depression, anxiety, loneliness, and anticipation. The urge to smoke is probably a combination of some of these emotions. When you feel a personal need or unsatisfied emotions, you long for the company of your friend, the cigarette. Think about this. Try to understand where your urges to smoke come from. At different times and in different situations the urge to smoke rides on different emotions, but every emotion is just that. It is a feeling that is only a suggestion and it comes quickly out of the blue. In Dr. Goleman's book *Emotional Intelligence: Why It Can Matter More Than IQ*, he describes how and why this happens. The emotional suggestions come through the limbic system of the brain whereas the rational part of the brain originates in the cerebral cortex. Emotional signals come much faster, and they get to your consciousness before the rational ones do. So the first thing you feel is the urge. It is alone and it strikes you without warning. As your habit grows, the urge can become like the order of a drill sergeant who commands, "Do it." However, the emotionally intelligent person knows that he or she outranks the sergeant. Imagine yourself in that situation. Think of what you might tell that sergeant, and then tell your habit in the most direct and forceful terms to settle back and never try that again.

CHAPTER 6

The Joys of Freedom

Have you ever watched a bird in flight? Some of these creatures are truly amazing. Some can fly across the ocean, obviously nonstop, with only the wind, their wings, and their muscles to power them. Hawks, catching warm updrafts, can float for hours circling high above the ground just looking for movement below. Large groups of geese fly in formation, constantly talking back and forth and cooperating with each taking its turn breaking the wind for the others. Crows are my favorites, as I have learned they are among the most intelligent of animals. I have heard crows talk, and their voices are as clear as that of any human. Videos show crows fashioning and using tools to retrieve food in challenging situations. And there are studies that have proven that crows pass learning from one generation to the next. They do all this with tiny bird brains that also know how to fly and navigate in three dimensions. It would be good to be able to learn what they are thinking and what other things they could be taught. But this is not about bird watching, at which I am just getting started. This is about the joy of freedom, and I thought birds soaring through the air might be an inspiration. Poets have assumed the same and have left us with expressions that try to glimpse some of that joy. I remember one of Shakespeare's sonnets which we read in high school. I think I can write it fairly accurately. This is how I remember it:

> When in disgrace with fortune and men's eyes
> I all alone beweep my outcast state,
> and trouble deaf heaven with my bootless cries,
> and look upon myself and curse my fate.

Wishing me like to one more rich in hope
Featured like him, like him with friends possessed
Desiring this man's art and that man's scope
With what I most enjoy contented least.

Yet in this state myself almost despising
Haply I think on thee,
and then my state, like to the lark at break of day arising
from sullen earth, sings hymns at heaven's gate.

For thy sweet love remembered such wealth brings
That then I scorn to change my state with kings.

The poet tells that reflection of his girl friend's love changes his spirits from self-despising to one that sings hymns at heaven's gate. The lark soars skyward filled with joy. There's not too much to a lark save strong wings, a sweet song, a heart of joy, and the desire to make that joy known to heaven and Earth. Would that we could feel that way! Freedom allows the bird to have joy and want to sing it out. Birds soar and dive to feel the thrill and joy of freedom. A smoker stands there watching, a prisoner and slave to his habit. In prison a person is not free but rather in servitude or slavery. Strange as it may seem, some smokers have accepted their fate. Like hostages who experience "the Stockholm syndrome," expressing empathy and positive feelings for their captors, they feel comfortable with their habit. It won't let them go, but in an unbelievably grand gesture they say, "That's okay." They think they can do without the joy of freedom as long as their friend (cigarettes) is there with them. This is twisted thinking and is strange and sad to give up so much for nothing more than nebulous smoke.

We need to emphatically tell smokers that they can get free, and with freedom they can know true joy. True joy is not necessarily a life of complete and exclusive joy. Ex-smokers can still have their trials and tribulations, but at the same time they can know true joy. As the poet says, his spirit goes like the lark to the gate of heaven. Joy is a spiritual state and, just like a physical state, you cannot truly experience it unless you can appreciate where you are. People on journeys have known joy just to see another milestone passed. If the journey is hard, the feeling may be more relief than joy, but it still has the component of personal success.

However, with smoking cessation, each day you feel better and stronger, and all the while your problems grow smaller. In a spiritual sense, you do experience joy if you understand and appreciate what you are accomplishing and why you are doing it. When you become a nonsmoker the reflection that you have made a positive permanent improvement in your lifestyle can afford a sense of true joy. You enhance that feeling with the knowledge that you are physically feeling better, mentally a lot clearer, and emotionally a lot stronger. Reflecting on these accomplishments, you might feel the joy and want to join in with the lark singing that hymn. This is not just hype. You can actually experience true joy. Joy will come when you allow it to come and recognize it for what it is. When you first decide to walk away from your smoking habit that could be a moment when the feeling of joy comes to you. It's not overwhelming joy, but it is a feeling that I have done something that I've wanted to do for a long time, and even though I don't know how this will turn out, I have decided to step out and try it. It's a positive move toward a real goal. It's bold in the sense that you know there will be temptations, but you have decided to do it anyway. With only this you can start to feel good about yourself. And now you can do something that you would not have been able to do minutes ago. You can plan and ready yourself for the next step. Welcome to the game. You know people who have given up smoking. Imagine you are walking in their shoes. Will you walk as boldly as they did? Take heart. That first step may be the hardest, and you have gotten over that one. If you falter now, you know you can and will make up your mind to go back to that first step as quickly as you can. It's not a question now of "can you," it's only a matter of time when you will break free. Realize this and let the joy pull you toward your goal.

PART TWO: WORKSHOP

A Note to the Reader

This is the working section of the book. In this section you will find a seven-step process to becoming a nonsmoker. I wrote this to be an easy, upbeat read, and I hope you find it to be an easy path to follow. In the ACS's "Guide to Quitting Smoking" and in many other places, it is recommended that you have an elaborate plan to follow before you begin to quit smoking (American Cancer Society 2011). Apparently, this is to concentrate your mind on the necessity of thoroughly planning and taking seriously all the steps to follow. I assume the purpose of this is that you will have the very best chance to be successful. Taking pains to give yourself every opportunity to be successful certainly sounds like a good idea. However, the facts might lead you to consider a different approach. The success rate for first attempts is quite low, and breaking completely free from smoking may take many attempts. As I see it, the tactic for a teacher or coach would be to encourage people to get started and make an attempt and, if not successful, then be prepared to try again as soon as possible. Imagine if you were in a group of people on a frozen lake. Perhaps you were ice fishing. Late in the afternoon the clouds darken, the wind get colder and stronger, and it starts to rain. There's a nice, warm, comfortable shelter some distance away. Would you spend some time thinking about working on your stride so you could get there on the first try without falling? Children would take off running. Most of them would fall but would quickly learn that it really didn't hurt. They would get up quickly and continue running, keeping their eyes on the goal. I think the children have the right idea and to them it would all be fun. Quitting smoking can be likened to running for that shelter. The ice and the distance to the shelter is a hazard that is similar to your smoking habit. You and the children face a dangerous storm if you do not get out of the way. They impulsively start to run, knowing that is the fastest way to escape danger. What they find out along the way is that it can actually be fun. In the very same way, you can discover that quitting smoking can be fun. I will mention this several times to help you work it into your beliefs.

It really doesn't take a lot of planning to *not do* something. Smoking is a contrived habit, while not smoking is natural. Recall the statistic that only 4 to 7 percent of attempts to quit are successful, and that it may take eight to ten attempts to get away from smoking completely. Better get started now. There are no fees or application papers to fill out. All you have to do is not smoke. *It really is as easy as that.* And remember that you spend much more time *not* smoking than you do smoking, and during those times you are not suffering. It requires nothing to try. Go for it! The withdrawal symptoms will probably be milder than you think. They can feel similar to flu symptoms and, if they truly bother you, you can seek medical advice. As I mentioned before, you can also try to sleep it off. What is the price or the cost for failure? Absolutely nothing! Trying and failing puts you way ahead of those who never try. When you fail, you can see where you went off course, and you can make plans to try again. That is when I recommend that you come back to this working section. Go through the workshop as a coach would go through the drills at halftime. Read each section out loud to yourself with emphasis. Tell yourself that if you would only pay attention to these details, you could be successful. Then go back out there and try again with renewed determination. Another helpful ballgame analogy is: when you fail, the coach calls time out, calls you over, and explains what you are doing wrong and how to do it right. The game never ends until you quit smoking for good.

The reason I call this a nonsmoking workshop is because the word "workshop" conjures up the notion of doing something. It might introduce some tools that will help you get the job done and guide you through the process of using those tools. The object of this workshop is to get your "buy in" to the fact that tools will help you give up smoking. In the following part there are specific tools that you can adjust for your particular situation. You can take these tools and use them to do something, in the first case, to quit smoking. However, the idea behind the use of tools can be found to be useful for other purposes, and that is an added bonus.

Terminology:
Smoker: one who routinely smokes cigarettes
Ex-smoker: one who has given up smoking
Nonsmoker: one who does not smoke and is never tempted to smoke

STEP 1 Make a Decision to Quit Smoking

You may think you have made the decision to stop smoking. You are attending this nonsmoking workshop; isn't that proof? While attending a workshop may provide you with an incentive, it is not proof that you have actually made a decision to quit smoking. Let us examine this in more detail. In everyday experience we see that some people make a decision to do something, and some are successful while others are not. Have you ever wondered why? In all probability there are many reasons. However, one of the most important might be in the planning that went into making the decision. Take, for instance, the decision to give up smoking. Do you just want to say, "I'm going to quit smoking," and then go out and wait for the first temptation and try to fight it off with "willpower"? That is one tactic and, for some, it has been successful. For many others it has been successful for a period of time, but they eventually fall back into the smoking habit again. Perhaps part of the problem was inadequate planning. If you are going to a new destination it is advisable to plan your trip. Now part of making the decision to quit smoking is agreeing to prepare for the temptations that will arise. The decision to quit is an act of the will; however, it does not necessarily take a lot of willpower. Quitting can be easy if you prepare, but much harder if you do not prepare. The rub here is that many people fail to prepare, and they do this deliberately. They have not really made a decision to quit. They have made a decision to *try* to quit. There is a difference, and you should realize what you must do to be successful. It is easy if you want to, but only you can want to.

Nobody can give up smoking for you. And nobody can give you the determination to do it. Your determination is required. Consider an analogy. Imagine a little girl getting up the courage to dive into a swimming pool. If she has the determination, she will probably make a pretty good dive. If she is not ready and tries to hold back it will probably not be a good dive, and the effort it takes to try will be much greater. Not only is it not successful, it is also much harder. But if she feels she doesn't have the courage, she might sit on the edge of the pool and dangle her legs in the water. This gives her time to truly make the decision and also to think about how she will actually do it. So the following two factors go into this:

1. Developing the courage to try
2. Working over in your mind just how to do it

And you need to determine this is what you want to do. As a test you can ask yourself the following questions:

- Do you really want to do this for the long haul?
- Would you like to think of yourself as a smoker or an ex-smoker?
- Are you willing to let go?
- If you make a decision to stop smoking and it is successful, will you be pleased and accept the result?

If there is any hesitancy, you can expect your quest to give up smoking will be much harder. It would probably be a good idea to go "dangle your legs in the water" and work over your own intentions.

If you try to quit and you fail, the problem will probably be (maybe has been) in the inadequacy of the plan. Specifically in not planning and working out beforehand how you will handle the temptations to smoke and, more strategically, how you will conquer your habit. Making a decision to quit smoking involves making a plan. It has been said that getting over a bad habit is not a decision; it is a process.

This workshop explains how to use specific tools to help you quit smoking. Using these tools will help you develop a plan to quit smoking. The process is a guide for what to do and outlines the steps that keep you involved in the process. It very much includes what to do if you backslide. If you keep to the process, it will guide you back to the right track. A relapse is not necessarily a failure. However, you need to evaluate how and why you relapsed, and use that information to see where in the process you need to put more effort and planning. Then armed with new plans and always staying aware of your previous success, you can look forward to getting back in the game. It may take a couple of times, but each completed step is your success, and with each step you gain confidence. It is like perfecting that dive and experiencing the exhilaration that goes with that success. Stick to the right basics and what you thought was going to be difficult can turn out to be fun and easy.

STEP 2 Do Not Give Up Smoking!

This may at first sound to be at cross-purposes to what we want to accomplish, but don't tune me out just yet. I smoked a pack a day for twenty years, and I know what I am talking about. I am going to present a scenario, and please listen to see if it sounds familiar. I'll bet you have been through this many times.

Somewhere along the line you consented to try a single puff from a cigarette. It probably was not pleasant, but somehow you got through it. Knowing it was not a pleasant experience and not finding any pleasure in smoking, what in the world led you to try a second puff? Only you can answer that. It might have been a challenge to see how other people got through the unpleasantness and got to the enjoyment. Anyway, you did it. And then did it again and again. Congratulations! Now the realization that you are a smoker has slipped into and taken up residence in your personality. You identify yourself as a smoker, and now there are consequences. As a smoker your subconscious brain understands that there is a rhythm to smoking. Twenty cigarettes in a sixteen- to eighteen-hour day is a little more than one cigarette per hour. Your subconscious brain keeps track. When the experience of smoking is overdue, it sends a signal. You become conscious of the fact that it has been over two hours since you have had a cigarette. Well, if it is inconvenient, you override the message and go on about your business. But your subconscious "clock" keeps running. A while later another signal is sent. Then you realize that it is even longer since you last had a cigarette. This keeps up until at last you get a chance to smoke, and then the subconscious clock is reset. What is addiction? It is largely being bombarded with these signals. The signals don't stop. Eventually you give in and smoke. Then to your great relief the messages stop. But no! Hell no! The only thing that has happened is that the clock has been reset. You are not free; you are just on another pulse. Realize that your addiction is very largely mental.

When you try to quit, you might think it is not fair. The state of your composure when compared to that of a nonsmoker is definitely not fair. You want to quit smoking, but the signals keep coming. And if you ignore them, they can begin to cause withdrawal symptoms such as headache, nausea, nervousness, and anxiety. Thus there are both physical and mental components to your addiction. To overcome addiction it is a good idea to consider the components separately. Physical addiction is caused by the action of nicotine in the body and brain. The nicotine molecule in the blood passing through the brain, because of its size and shape, can act like a neurotransmitter and cross into the brain where it can stimulate a pleasure receptor. The stimulated receptor can release chemicals that produce pleasure or well-being. However, the smokers that I interviewed, as well as myself, would not say the primary response was pleasure. The first puff from a cigarette was satisfying. You felt you had done the right thing to make yourself feel better. However, it was more relief than pleasure. Furthermore, the satisfaction was not enhanced as you continued smoking. The reader can be the judge as to whether the following is a good description of how they feel when smoking. When you smoke you get a little kick with each puff. That little kick is barely noticeable. Your heart rate and blood pressure may spike up a little, and maybe you experience some other physical symptoms, but they pass very quickly. After taking another puff, you get another little kick. Soon you come to the end of the cigarette, and the accumulation of all these little kicks has not had any effect on you. They're gone. You are the same person that you always were. You are not in some altered state. You can still drive a car, operate machinery, speak, think, and act normally. People are not afraid to have you around children. They know and expect you to be normal. Very little of your body chemistry has changed. There are physical effects of smoking on the respiratory system, but these are not addictive. My son was a critical care nurse at a hospital where alcoholics and drug addicts were taken. Some of these people were very sick. However, the standard treatment for every one of them started in the intensive care unit (ICU) where they received intravenous medications. That is because there is a risk of seizures and heart attacks from a stone-cold withdrawal. Their body chemistry had been altered by the abuse of drugs and alcohol. The effects are long lasting. Conversely, nicotine produces a little spike and then it washes out of the system very quickly. You know that one puff does not build on the next puff. How quickly the "joy" goes away! And as ex-smokers will testify, the physical effects are short lived, much shorter than would be expected if the source of addiction was primarily in the physical chemistry of the body.

There are nicotine receptors in the brain, and they contribute to the physical source of addiction to smoking. However, the question of how strong is the physical addiction and how long does it continue to bother those who quit smoking needs to be clarified. It is a fact that nicotine washes out of the body fairly quickly and is usually gone in three to four days. The withdrawal symptoms last about the same length of time (American Cancer Society 2011). Most ex-smokers will affirm that after the withdrawal symptoms go away, the physical desire for a cigarette does too.

There is another difference between smoking and the addiction to "hard drugs." Smoking does not alter your mind or put you in another state. The addiction to hard drugs includes a longing for that altered state as a means to escape reality. None of this comes into play with smoking.

Mental addiction is something else, and it can be very strong. It is important that you realize that addiction is much harder to overcome if you do not understand it. Lacking understanding leads to fighting the wrong battle. Of course you will not be successful there. Your energy will be dissipated, and you will be discouraged by your lack of progress. Conversely, knowing what is happening and identifying the source of your problems gives you power. Knowledge is power. It helps you to devise ways to overcome your addiction.

STEP 3 Understanding Your Addiction

A. What are the Sources of Addiction?

The addiction to smoking has both physical and mental components. The physical components come from nicotine and the withdrawal symptoms that you often experience when you stop smoking. You have experienced withdrawal symptoms many times as a smoker. For a smoker who averages a cigarette every hour, withdrawal symptoms begin after four or five hours without a cigarette. Tiredness, dizziness, and possibly a headache will start to occur. The smoker knows that she needs a cigarette. This happens so often that people barely realize it, but these are, in fact, withdrawal symptoms.

The mental components result from your acceptance of the advertised claim that smoking brings relaxation and pleasure. One of the main goals of this book is to throw cold water on that false claim. When you take the bait and make the association, you store that idea in your subconscious mind. The emotional urge for a cigarette is fed to the conscious mind every time you get the feeling that you want some relaxation or pleasure. In the discussions to follow I refer to these emotional urges as temptations. The Workshop will argue that the association is false. You actually bring and realize the relaxation and pleasure by other means falsely accepting that they are brought by smoke and nicotine.

B. Overcoming Physical Addiction

A smoker is addicted to nicotine. When you smoke your heart rate and blood pressure go up, and maybe you become more alert. These are the little "kicks" I referred to earlier. *But is the addiction physical?*

You put up with several negative effects to get a few positive effects. But you are only very mildly physically addicted. Nicotine wears away quickly. If you never had nicotine again you would probably get a headache and be nervous and irritable for a time. But most likely you would not experience great physical stress or illness, and all of your bodily and mental functions would continue to work just fine. You are not greatly physically addicted! You and your doctors, in most cases, would not anticipate real problems and could assume that whatever physical addiction you had will wear away quickly. It is a good idea to prepare for any withdrawal you might experience by planning to do it when you will not be stressed with other things. Some good times might be on the weekend when you can sleep it off or when you are going to be active, as that will help take your mind off of the symptoms.

C. Understanding Mental Addiction

The mental addiction to smoking is from your subconscious mind sending signals that tell you it is time to light up a cigarette. Let us try to understand this in more detail. As I stated before, there are distinct parts in the human brain that deal with either emotional or cognitive (thinking) functions. The limbic system handles the emotional signals, and the response from this system has to be very fast. If you are suddenly in great danger, your life may depend on how quickly you respond. During highly stressful times, emotional signals can take over the brain. We have heard people under stress say they can not think straight. This is an accurate statement. In these situations, the limbic system has "hijacked" the brain (Goleman 1997). In less stressful situations it is still true that the emotional signals go very fast through the limbic system. When the signal telling you to smoke comes, it travels through the limbic system much faster than the same signal going through the cognitive system. This means that you feel the urge to smoke before you have had a chance to think about it. Using imaging techniques they can actually see certain parts of the brain "light up" before other parts. You want to smoke before you even know why. If you seize on that, the emotion can hijack the brain. You can actually think of nothing else but getting what the emotional system is signaling. This is mental addiction.

D. Breaking Free from Mental Addiction

You have identified yourself as a smoker. As such, your subconscious mind keeps track. Its job is to see that your fasting from smoking does not go on too long. It is easy to see that it is on the job. Now you realize how unfair it is. Imagine finishing a cigarette and, to your great relief, the "overdue" messages have stopped. But now the clock is reset and starts running again, so that in one hour you are going to be bombarded with more signals. For a nonsmoker at that time there will be no signals or messages telling him it's time to light up again. It's so unfair. He can go on forever without the slightest bother. You will be bombarded regularly until you give in. And give in you probably will. The messages, in a manner of speaking, add up. After a long fast there is great relief when you finally give in and light up. This causes people to conclude that they are smokers, and that it is futile to try to quit smoking, because it is such a relief when you go back to smoking again. You believe you would not experience this relief if you were not meant to be a smoker, and there is nothing you can do about it.

That is dead wrong! Only you can identify yourself as a smoker. The opposite is also true. Only you can identify yourself as a nonsmoker. You have the control that you *allow* yourself to have. Identifying yourself as a nonsmoker can make your quest to give up smoking a hundred times easier and, best of all, you can make it fun. The messages from your subconscious mind will still come periodically; however, they do not necessarily have to tell you to light up a cigarette. A woman who was a smoker read the write-up of this nonsmoking workshop. She was impressed and asked me if I thought it would work. I said, "Yes." Then she told me that she was afraid to try it. She had been overweight for a long time and was not successful in her attempts to lose weight. Finally, she had an operation and her weight went down to a much healthier level. She said if she gave up smoking, she thought she would eat a lot more and put the weight back on. Worries are a double-edged sword. They can warn you of danger, but they can also keep you from finding golden rewards. Woody Hayes was a great coach of the Ohio State football team. Ohio State was good, but maybe they could have been even better. In football today, passing the ball is required of a good offense. But Woody said he did not like to pass, because two of the three possible outcomes are negative—an incomplete pass results in the loss of a down, and an interception stops your offense completely. However, the third one, a completed pass, can be hugely positive. You have to have good plans and the confidence in yourself to go ahead and try. The messages will come until you become a nonsmoker. The quicker you become a nonsmoker, the sooner the messages will stop. Two good strategies to help you make plans are as follows:

1. Be active. When you are involved doing something, you may not hear the subconscious messages that urge you to smoke. However, many people have hobbies, and when doing these hobbies they really

like to smoke. The best advice is to do something that helps you avoid the temptations.

2. Change the message. This is a great tactic. Convert the message into something you would really like to do. Choose well. The messages come at any time, so choose something you can do at any time. You could say a prayer or maybe just think about something pleasant. You could try to remember something, solve a mental puzzle, or remind yourself how strong you are and how much you enjoy these little challenges. This is not something that needs to go on forever. The messages stop when you become a nonsmoker. However, it can be the start of a good practice just to remind yourself to think of something positive, or something you would like to remember or do on a regular basis. Good habits beget more good habits.

Remember, no matter how bad your habit is, you are still *not* smoking a lot more time than you are actively smoking. During these nonsmoking intervals, remind yourself that you are a nonsmoker. Think of it as throwing a switch from on to off. You are who you say you are. If you tell yourself you are not a smoker-that you are a nonsmoker, eventually you become one. Now for the good part: identifying yourself as a nonsmoker gives you the following experiences that smokers do not have:

- You can enjoy fresh air more.
- Food may taste better.
- You are free of those demanding signals telling you to smoke.
- You can join the millions of ex-smokers and nonsmokers.
- You can be thrilled about your change. *You have control.*

How do you free yourself from mental addiction? Tell yourself as often as you can that you are a nonsmoker. What you are doing at the present time does not matter. Even if you are actively smoking at the time, you can identify yourself as a nonsmoker. What you're doing at the present time is not the question. The true identity is what you will be and what you will work to be until you achieve it. Notice the difference. You are not a smoker who has gone on the wagon or who is quitting. You are not a muscleman or superhuman who is standing up to those messages that you must smoke. You are a nonsmoker. You have simply made the decision to stop, and you have either pushed the switch over, or you are working to get it into the nonsmoking position. You will know when it is there, because the messages will stop. The silence will fill your consciousness. You will be thrilled and bask in the silence and relief. You will look back for the rest of your days and remember that the messages stopped and what a great feeling it was to get free of such a crippling condition. The very best part is feeling and knowing that you controlled the whole process.

STEP 4 Becoming a Nonsmoker

You are who you think you are. This is true in general. And we can use it for a guide. Of course, there are times when it is not true. We all know stories, jokes, and cases of mental delusion. But in this context, what do we mean when we say, "You are who you think you are"?

Your consciousness tells you who you are. Tell yourself often that you are a nonsmoker. Doing that makes the messages stop sooner. Keep it up, and have some fun with it. Previously, when you got the message to smoke, you interrupted what you were doing and took the time to light up and smoke a cigarette. You looked forward to smoking. Now that you are a nonsmoker there are many things you can look forward to doing. Use this opportunity to do something you like to do or would like to learn. One planning technique is to choose something that you would like to do. It doesn't have to be something you know or do at the present time. You will be reminded on a schedule. Pick something you would like to enjoy. When the messages to smoke come, you can do one of the following things.

- Do it.
- Practice it.
- Learn about it.
- Think about it.
- Memorize it.
- Plan for it.
- Remember it.
- Pray for it.
- Study it.
- Get involved in it.

For example, shuffle your feet and pretend you are dancing. This is something you can do mentally to change the message to something more positive. Make this task something you enjoy. Have fun doing this. You are taking control. Grab the wheel and make it go where you want it to go.

One thing that might come up is the urge to eat. This just replaces one enjoyment with another enjoyment. So far that is good, but there are drawbacks. When you feel the urge to indulge, you might not be able to eat something right away. So you put it off. The next time the urge could be a double-barreled blast that tells you to smoke *and* to eat. Eating even just a little every time you get a signal to smoke would not be healthful, wise, or even practical. So you have, in effect, doubled your difficulties. It is better to change the message into a mental activity that you can do at any time and as privately as you wish. People may see you smile, but that can be your secret.

Okay, here is a little test. What is wrong with substituting the urge to eat for the satisfaction of smoking a cigarette? One problem is that they are very closely tied together in your mind. Many times after you finish eating, you like to enjoy a cigarette. So by eating you are asking for a strong temptation to light up a cigarette. It does not get you away from smoking; it drags you toward it. On another level, you understand that they are both emotional signals. Substituting one for the other is childish in that "if I can't have one I'll insist on having the other." It's not the way to grow up, and it doesn't really work. You usually find you still want the thing you did not have. The temptation is probably just delayed. And the final reason, as this workshop teaches, is that you definitely do not want to feel you are being deprived. If you feel that you are fasting and this is difficult, you are not going to get away from your habit. You are actually holding onto it. You really have to understand and buy-in to the idea that you are on a mission to change something that is not good for something that is good. The goal of nonsmoking has to trump the temptation of smoking. When you get this down, you will not have to push your temptations away. Your goals will pull you forward. In fact, you can lean back and let them take you for a ride. Again, look at this as an opportunity, which it truly is, and then pick something that makes you happy and find ways to enjoy it as often as you enjoyed a cigarette. Just be careful that it is not something that will connect you to smoking. Exclusivity is the key here.

STEP 5 What to Do if You Slip or Relapse

A slip is when you smoke one or two cigarettes. A relapse is when you start smoking regularly again. Do not let yourself get discouraged. Discouragement is easy and might even be tempting. But you have to catch yourself. Know and remember that having a slip or a relapse can be part of the process. But the other part of the process is to quit again. Remember, it may take several attempts, and this is just one of them. Just get back up and start again as soon as possible. Focus on becoming a nonsmoker and how you will feel when you discover that you can do what you want to do. Suppose you have been a nonsmoker for awhile, and then old friends, relatives, a lover, or someone else drops by for a visit. For some reason, they offer you a cigarette and, although you know you should decline, you fail to do that. In situations like these, how can you politely decline? You can simply say, "No thanks, I no longer smoke." You do not need to make a big fuss about it. You can just let it go; the quicker the better.

There may be a different scenario in which you started smoking again. So what? Nothing major has changed. You have smoked lots of cigarettes. You can start over and identify yourself as a nonsmoker even though you started smoking again. When you start to get messages from your subconscious mind, tell yourself that these signals are not welcome. Tell your subconscious mind that you do not want to become a smoker again. Remind yourself that you enjoy being a nonsmoker. You made a decision that you are not going back. You are going forward. You will succeed if you keep identifying yourself as a nonsmoker.

You may remember times when you really enjoyed looking forward to smoking a cigarette. It might be helpful to analyze these instances to figure out what motivated you to smoke. How did that cigarette contribute to the enjoyment? It probably doesn't make sense. Most probably you have worked it into the scenario. It became your habit, but it is not really a necessary part of the enjoyment. If you removed smoking from the process, would the thing that you enjoy really change? No, of course it would not. You might feel a little less comfortable because you were used to smoking at this time. But with repetition, that will change and you will feel more comfortable. You ultimately have control over it. You can decide that you no longer need to smoke to have an enjoyable time. In fact, as nonsmokers can tell you and you can discover, smoking detracts from your enjoyment because it puts demands on you which can be a distraction. Undoubtedly you know this. Things can be so much simpler and every bit as enjoyable. Recall some of the times you felt you had to smoke when it was not convenient or even the right thing to do at the time. Then let yourself begin to realize that smoking has actually ruined many a good time with its incessant demands. Furthermore by accepting the suggestion that smoking brings relaxation and pleasure, you probably have foregone or postponed relaxation or pleasure because you couldn't smoke at that time. Some of these opportunities might have evaporated while you were waiting. This is a huge social penalty for a smoker. While you wait for a time to light up a cigarette, a nonsmoker is ready to enjoy pleasure spontaneously as it comes up.

STEP 6 How to Handle the Tough Times.

The problems covered in this step and the preceding one go hand in hand. Often when times get tough a person quitting smoking might succumb to a temptation and start smoking again. The combination of tough times causing the person to smoke again can result in an endless feedback cycle. For this reason I discuss these problems separately in order to help you face them separately. The tactic of a fighter is to face one assailant at a time, keeping the others at bay. Tough times are the expressions of mental withdrawal symptoms.

1.   Occurrence of tough times

> You should think and reflect carefully when temptations are most likely to gain entry into your psyche. Write down the circumstances when you are most vulnerable. Keep the list and add to it the tough times you experience. These are the times you need to be on guard, and be able to recognize threats, and realize when they are not being cleanly rejected.
> It is important not to dwell in tough times. Some indications of trouble brewing are:
>
> a. When you feel you are not making progress
>
> > Ups and downs will occur and should be expected. You can enjoy the ups. It's the downs that you have to be prepared to tackle. As with any challenges some of the times you will handle them easily; some will be a real battle. Make an effort to be cognizant of how the temptation got started, how it got to be a problem, and how you handled it. These struggles are a good learning experience. Look at them as such. I remember the great boxer Sugar Ray Leonard telling an interviewer that he can't wait for the fight to start.

When you are prepared you can easily face the temptations.

b. When the thought of smoking creeps into your mind

> The thought of smoking does not occur to a nonsmoker. For a person quitting smoking they will feel it is natural to smoke at certain times. At first it will take a noticeable reaction to reject the temptation to light up. You learned to smoke; you will have to learn not to. No one wants to go back to first grade, but that may be what is required. The smart thing is to learn fast and enjoy the feeling of going fast. Occasionally, you will find that a temptation will stick in your mind. This is the time to realize that you are in danger. You will have to take action to fight off the temptation.

c. When you start to doubt that you will be successful.

> This is a sign of real trouble. You can not go far doubting yourself. You may have already started smoking again. If so, go back the previous step covering a slip or relapse. If you continue doubting go back to the start and begin again.

d. When you would not be surprised to see yourself smoking again

> At this point you are a smoker. You have to start over with making a decision to quit smoking.

2. What to do when you are in trouble.

> The first thing is to get over the immediate temptation. After that you can get help and try to figure out how to avoid temptations in the future. It would be wise to collect some thoughts on how you will do these things, because tough times will come, and you probably will do better if you are prepared. A list of actions you should be prepared to implement is as follows:
>
> > a. Get over the immediate temptation.
> > b. Get help.
> > c. Get rested and refreshed.
> > d. Look to the future. Do you want to be a nonsmoker?
> > e. Do some nonsmoker things that you enjoy.
> > f. Study ways to avoid temptations in the first place.
> > g. Enjoy your status of being a nonsmoker.

STEP 7 Enjoy Your Freedom

We started out mindful of what influenced us to smoke. It was certain pleasures that we thought smoking induced. However there are many other pleasures that are better experienced without smoking. When you stop smoking it is a good time to start enjoying some of the following pleasures:

a. Doing breathing exercises. When you take deep breaths, it purges your lungs and increases your energy.
b. Getting actively involved in walking, gardening, favorite projects, bicycling, swimming, skiing, skating, dancing, or whatever you like to do.
c. Beginning or getting back to your hobbies, such as traveling, or other activities.
d. Enjoying the new feeling of being in control.
e. Being thankful that all irritating side-effects are gone.
f. Realize your freedom from all the business about smoking.
g. Realize that cigarettes do not add to the pleasure of your favorite things. You will discover you can enjoy these things as much or more as a nonsmoker. You will feel more relaxed as you become more confident.
h. Being relieved knowing that you have one less thing to worry about.

Cigarettes did not empower you. You are the one with the power. You gave some of that power away, and taking it back puts you in greater control. Smile often, knowing that you have made it. You can relax and think more clearly without those demanding interruptions. You can feel more self confident knowing you are in control and have broken away from an ensnarling habit. Remember, it is important to enjoy your freedom!

PART THREE: TOOLS AND SKILLS

Tools to Help You Put Your Smoking Habit to Rest

Humankind has made progress, in part, by the continuous development of better and better tools. These implements have made work easier and quicker. When it comes to trying to quit smoking the proper tools can make the job easier and faster. Therefore, do not skip over this segment. Put some work into it, and discover that you can fashion tools that are fun to use. It is fun as you realize how easy it can be to cut through habits that were tough. The way tools are designed is by understanding the forces in order to focus the effort in the right places. If the material is hard or tough, you make the tool harder and sharper. In this way hard jobs become easy. You get through the job faster and feel good about doing so. And you feel good about yourself. You know you understand the problems and the way to get through them. You take pride in your accomplishments.

A toolmaker thinks about what exactly needs to be done. He then makes sketches, thinking through each step, and visualizing how to use the tool and how it will work. The first step is to focus on the work itself. You need to determine what exactly needs to be done. You can get confused and lost in the overall project. The worker needs to focus. Do you want to build a house? If so, that defines the overall objective, but it does not say what has to be done at a particular moment. Maybe you just need to cut a board to size or drive a nail. At times you need to put away thoughts about the larger picture and concentrate on the details.

For smoking cessation you want to make your desire for cigarettes go away. But it just may be that at the present time your focus needs to be on substituting your chosen "good" thought or action for the temptation to light up a cigarette. The house that you build or the project that you take on will depend on how well you do these tasks and how well they go together. This book is a blueprint. If you do the individual steps well, you will put together a good project, be successful in stopping your smoking habit, and put a good habit in its place.

There are a large variety of tools. There are machine tools and hand tools. They can be very simple or quite complicated. However, they all have one thing in common, and that is they were made to get some job done more easily. Hand tools are common and perhaps the word conjures up the thought of them. But there is a much greater variety of tools, and what I offer you are tools to help you understand, see, and navigate your way away from your smoking habit. Some will say these tools are mere suggestions. In my mind that is like saying a hammer is a mere object. A tool is what you use it for and what you make of it. You can use the tools presented here to overcome a demanding habit. They can help gain perspective and stay focused throughout the struggle. They can be mere suggestions to some, but you can take them to heart, memorize them, and depend on them for guidance and support.

When you read this section on tools and skills, then you can begin to appreciate the utility they can bring to your struggle. You have read about addiction to nicotine. There are nicotine supplements, and these fall into the category of tools. My argument is that the tools presented here can help you overcome your habit much faster and that you become stronger in contrast to other aids that may make you weaker by using them. In addition, just as a hammer or screwdriver can be used for many jobs, you will discover that the tools you develop for getting rid of a bothersome habit will be useful for other tasks. Let us get to work developing these tools so that you can put them to good use.

Tools for Each Step

Tools for Step 1. Making a Decision to Quit Smoking

The best tool for making a decision is to look to the future. Do not get involved with the details. Time goes on without your pushing it, and you cannot stop it. The future will come. The only thing you can do is guide it a little bit. So are you shaping the future to be what you want? Think of it as a machine winding up a rope. You cannot stop the machine or control the speed. All you can do is to try to guide the rope on the mandrel. You have only a little force compared to the power of the machine. The reel will turn at a set speed. You can guide the rope doing a good job or you can let it go. The way to do a good job is to guide the rope by looking a fairly long way out. If you try to guide the rope too close to the reel, you will not have time to react if a little loop or any small disturbance comes along. You will lose control and the rope will go any which way. You then have to work harder to gain control, which can be a losing battle. You can spend a great deal of effort and still have a mess on your hands. The same is true about driving a car. If you try to steer by looking down at the road, you will not be able to keep the car on the road, and you will expend a lot of effort trying. The best way is to look a certain distance ahead. So when you are planning what you want to do, look to the future. Not the very distant future but at least a year out. At the end of the year you will have spent some energy trying to make yourself into the person you want to be. To make things easier and to have as much control as you can look a year ahead and use the following thoughts to motivate your efforts:

> a. I will keep my focus on this project.
> b. I will increase my desire to quit.
> c. I will increase my determination.
> d. I will face the fact that I will never smoke again.
> e. I have confidence that this is something that is going to happen.
> f. I am excited to be in this challenge.
> g. I cannot wait for progress and to see this happening.

Look a year ahead, but be mindful of how the rope is lying on the reel. If things are going smoothly enjoy the control you are exerting. *Be proud and happy.* Keep going the way you are doing it. If, however, the rope is not laying down smoothly, most of the time a small adjustment in your control can correct the problem. *Do not panic and do not give up.* You have already made progress and a slight adjustment will make things go smoothly again. Do not try to reach back and smooth things out on the reel. What is gone is gone. There is no problem. Focus on the future. Temptations and setbacks are made to stir up your determination. Go with it. Let your determination build up. A nonsmoking you is developing. Smile and be glad.

Tools for Step 2. Do Not Give Up Smoking

In step 1, the emphasis is on looking ahead. Giving up something keeps bringing you back to the present. You draw a line from the day you quit and measure to the present. Most people can tell you how many days it has been since they last had a cigarette. They are just fasting. They are probably not intending to quit, but merely putting some time in before they light up again. Go back to step 1 and you can see the difference between just giving it up for a little while as opposed to planning ahead and looking forward to making a permanent change. Do you want to fight yourself all the time, or do you want to cruise? Lift yourself up and look down on the situation. One scenario is that you will see someone who, if not really happy, is at least excited about making progress. The other person is fighting off the temptation to light up every hour, and worst of all, he feels that he is depriving himself of something that will ease his tension. Therein is the difficulty in giving up smoking. You tried to give up smoking and now you realize that you just made life difficult for yourself. You failed because you were fighting yourself. There is hardly a winner in that situation, and there is no need to do it.

Try to realize and understand that you are not giving up anything. There is nothing negative about what you are doing. Ex-smokers do not long for a cigarette. Quite the contrary, most of them hate smoking and it really comes naturally. After breaking away from the "pleasure" of smoking, one sees there really was little or no pleasure in it, and the negatives vastly outnumber the positives. Nonsmokers hate to see others still trapped in the smoke, and they think of smoke and react as you would to smoke from another fire. It is obnoxious and harmful; there is nothing to like about it. Let these ideas soak into your mind. Write down how you would tell someone dear to you the dangers and negatives of smoking. You can be your own best teacher. This helps you develop the right frame of mind. Smoking is not your friend. It has held you back from developing further. It has entrapped you and hounded you. "Did you forget your cigarettes today? Better check." It has cost you and taken its toll on your health, opportunity, friendships, and personal relationships. What is there to like about that?

Write down the one thing you most dislike or regret that smoking has caused in your life. Come back to this note occasionally and see if you can think of other things that you hate about smoking. *You are going away from, but you are not "giving up" smoking.*

The following thoughts can help remind you that you do not want to "give up" smoking:

    a. Giving up is temporary.
    b. Have you ever been successful for the long run giving up anything?
    c. You gave up smoking before, but now you're back smoking.
    d. Do you want to fight off temptations all your life?

Bob Newhart did a comedy routine where he was an investor sponsoring Sir Walter Raleigh's expedition to the new world. He calls Sir Walter Raleigh from England to question him about what he found in the New World. He is anticipating that the explorer found gold or similar riches he would bring back to make them rich. Walter Raleigh did not mention finding anything like that, so Bob Newhart asks him what he found. Walter Raleigh tells him, and Bob Newhart is repeating what he said as you do when talking on the phone. "Tobacco? What is that? It's a leaf? You have to dry it? Then you roll it up in paper?" This is really sounding crazy. He is wondering if Walter Raleigh has gone off his rocker. He asks, "Then what do you do with it? You light it with a match? Ha, ha. What do you do then? Stick it in your ear?"

Smoking is not something that you would think of right off the bat. It is a contrived habit. You will feel more natural and at ease without a cigarette burning in your hand. The Tool for Step 2 is to tell yourself often that you are not giving up anything. Rather you are doing something positive. Just say, "I need to make my smoking habit go away so I can be happy. And most importantly, I will not miss it."

Tools for Step 3. Understanding Your Addiction

After reading about physical addiction, I hope you have accepted the fact that your problems with quitting smoking do not come primarily from physical sources. If you are worried about this, go back and re-read the material about physical addiction. Then ask an ex-smoker you know how much trouble he or she had with physical addiction. As the person speaks, be mindful to separate the mental from the physical sources of addiction. Then ask the person how long the physical problems continued. Almost all ex-smokers will assure you that physical symptoms are an initial problem, but they quickly fade away and never come back.

To overcome physical addiction, tell yourself the following things:

     a. I am not seriously physically addicted.
     b. I am ready to meet these challenges.
     c. I can get over the physical demands to smoke.
     d. I can overcome these temporary challenges.

To work free from mental addiction, use the following tools to guide you:

     a. Mental addiction is a strong force, but understanding helps me to make plans and develop strategies.
     b. My habit is sustained only by letting my subconscious mind remind me that it is time to light up a cigarette.
     c. I created the habit. I can master it.
     d. I will talk to my habit as to a child. I will tell it that my needs and desires are the better way and the way I will go.
     e. Nonsmokers are not hounded by signals to smoke.
     f. Life would be so much easier if I did not have to contend with this all day long.
     g. I will work to stop or change the messages to smoke.

Tools for Step 4. Becoming a Nonsmoker.

Say to yourself, "This book has convinced me, and I now see that a large and persistent part of my addiction is a habitual response to signals from my subconscious mind." People can get addicted to seeking relaxation and pleasure, and they can be led to think they get that from smoking. They can even make it happen. That can be their way, but it is not the only way. Nonsmokers find relaxation and pleasure in much more pleasing ways. Choose one you like. When the urge to smoke comes, realize you can change that into a call to do something more pleasurable and rewarding. Don't waste the opportunity. When you become a nonsmoker the messages stop. Develop a good habit while you are still getting these signals on a timed schedule. Meditate or pray for help and it will come to you. Use the following ideas to help reinforce your determination:

Statements to Reinforce Your Determination

> a. I identify myself as a nonsmoker.
> b. I look forward to becoming a nonsmoker.
> c. Nonsmokers are not temped to smoke.
> d. I can anticipate and steer the signals to smoke toward a more positive goal.

Statements for becoming a nonsmoker.

> a. There are nonsmokers that I admire.
> b. I would like to be free like them.
> c. I think of myself as a nonsmoker.
> d. I plan, practice, and dream of becoming a nonsmoker.
> e. I find and substitute activities that I enjoy to replace the habit of smoking.
> f. I admire and imitate nonsmokers. During the day I practice being a nonsmoker by thinking and acting like one.
> g. I look forward and enjoy doing this.

Ask yourself the following questions:

a. How long will it take for me to become a nonsmoker?
b. As a nonsmoker, what would I say or feel if someone offered me a cigarette?
c. As a nonsmoker, what would I think or feel if my subconscious mind sent me a signal to light up?

Tools for Step 5. What to Do if You Slip or Relapse.

When you identify yourself as a nonsmoker, it will feel natural not to smoke. However, an occasion may come along during which you smoke a cigarette. Immediately remind yourself and say, "Remember that you are a nonsmoker." Tell yourself that what you just did was not worth it and, in fact, was ridiculous. Say, "I do not want to throw away all my efforts and the opportunities that getting free from smoking will provide." A true nonsmoker would never be in this position. Tell yourself the following things:

> a. Nothing has changed or been affected.
> b. I am still a nonsmoker.
> c. I will look into why I smoked or returned to smoking.
> d. I will make plans to get around doing that again.
> e. I will think and say that I stopped smoking on the original date.
> f. I affirm that I am a nonsmoker.
> g. I will not be tempted to go back to smoking.
> h. I will continue to work until I am a true nonsmoker.

Tools for Step 6. How to Handle the Tough Times

Times get tough only when you are unsure of yourself. If you keep questioning yourself, you can bet you will be tempted again. If that is what you want you can very easily get yourself into that position. However, if you really want to change, the temptations will be far less numerous and a lot easier to overcome. It is really your will, not your willpower that will solve this problem. Go back to Step 1 and reconsider your decision to quit smoking. Do you want to pause or do you want to quit? As the instructor would say, "Do not come back until you make up your mind." Know that nonsmokers do not have these tough times. The temptations will eventually go away and never come back. When you do decide to quit, the following thoughts will help make the tough times easier.

a. Most of the time temptations build slowly giving me time to prepare to battle them.
b. I need to be aware and vigilant in rejecting quickly any urge to smoke.
c. I cannot dwell on any attraction to smoking.
d. There are times when temptations are difficult, but realizing the source of the temptation helps in fighting it off.
e. This is a challenge I can work through.
f. I will keep quitting this horrible habit.
g. I am a nonsmoker for good.

Tools for Step 7. Enjoy Your Freedom

Congratulations on your success, but do not waste your new opportunities. You have taken a big step toward self improvement, but one step does not take you all the way. You are free from having a smoking habit, but realize that you could and should continue to improve yourself. There can be a better you. Go live it! Start there, but the whole idea is for you to keep going and improving. The following thoughts can help you in this quest:

> a. I enjoy doing this.
> b. I look ahead to see what else this process can do for me.
> c. I let other people and my friends see that I enjoy doing this.
> d. I find outlets and time for my new interests and things I want to do.
> e. I am free! Smoking has no holds on me.
> f. I feel good that I accomplished this myself.
> g. I am successful. My self confidence increases.
> h. I can do more good and be a better friend, because I am free of the shackles of smoking.

Review the Steps

1. Make a Decision to Quit Smoking
   a. Develop the courage to try
   b. Work over in your mind just how you will do it.
   c. Get determined that this is what you want to do.
2. Do Not Give Up Smoking
   a. You really can *enjoy* not smoking.
   b. Take a deep breath. Enjoy it.
   c. Every minute that you are not smoking is good for you and is a positive step toward your goal.
3. Understanding Your Addiction
   a. Withdrawal symptoms pass quickly and never return.
   b. Smokers get temptations to smoke; nonsmokers are free.
   c. It is your choice to be a nonsmoker. If you want to be one, you will be one.
4. Becoming a Nonsmoker
   a. Look forward to becoming a nonsmoker.
   b. Identify yourself as a nonsmoker.
   c. Practice the role of being a nonsmoker.
   d. Substitute something good for the urge to smoke.
5. What to Do if You Slip or Relapse
   a. Review why you smoked a cigarette.
   b. Make plans to avoid it in the future.
   d. Focus on the future.Forget the past.
   e. Start again as soon as possible.
6. How to Handle the Tough Times
   a. Tough times happen when I get depressed.
   b. I need to reject temptations cleanly.
   c. This is a challenge for me to work through.
   d. I will never quit quitting this horrible habit.
7. Enjoy Your Freedom
   a. I enjoy doing this.
   b. I am glad that I accomplished this myself.
   c. I can do more good and be a better friend.

Make a Pocket-Sized Laminate

Step 1.   The simplest decision is to say, "This is something that I am going to do."

Step 2.   I am not giving up anything. I am taking back control.

Step 3.   I will understand what addiction is and what it is not. I will control and redirect my mental addiction.

Step 4.   I will think of the easiest way and the way to have the most fun becoming a nonsmoker.

Step 5.   I know that a slip or a relapse is just a stumble along the way.

Step 6.   Tough times are a challenge for me to work through. I will persevere in quitting smoking.

Step 7.   When I break free, I will not waste the effort. I will enjoy my new life and newfound power to decide what I want.

Conclusions

1. The most important step is to make the decision to become a nonsmoker. It is your decision. It does not work by using willpower.
2. Determination makes this possible.
3. Smoking is a contrived habit. You will feel more natural when you do not smoke.
4. Plans to quit smoking need to include desire, determination, and acceptance of what is required. They should not be so elaborate that they delay your starting.
5. Success rates for individual attempts are low, but millions have successfully quit.
6. It is fine if it takes eight to ten attempts, as long as you do not give up.
7. When you fail, try again as soon as possible.
8. Physical addiction is short-lived. It will go away and never return.
9. Mental addiction resides in the rhythm of your smoking habit and in the feeling that smoking brings relaxation and pleasure.
10. The reasoned approach in this method can help dispel mental addiction.
11. The reasoned approach is cold turkey reinforced by the acceptance of well-thought-out arguments. It is combined with the determination to follow the seven simple steps until you are smoke-free.
12. Using the right approach can make quitting much easier.
13. There is an opportunity to substitute a good action for the urge to smoke.

References

American Cancer Society. "Guide to Quitting Smoking," 2011.
A free, online file that you can read and download at www.cancer.org

Daniel Goleman. 1997 *Emotional Intelligence: Why It Can Matter More Than IQ*. New York: Bantam Dell.

Mayer, John D., et al. 2001. "Emotional intelligence as a standard intelligence." *Emotion*, 1 (3): 232–242.

Salovey, Peter. 1997. "What is emotional intelligence?" Peter Salovey & David Sluyter, eds., *Emotional Development and Emotional Intelligence: Implications for Educators*. Pp. 3–31. New York: Basic Books.

Schachter, Neil, MD. 2003. *Life and Breath: The Breakthrough Guide to the Latest Strategies for Fighting Asthma and Other Respiratory Problems —At Any Age*. New York: Broadway Books.